Global Economics:
Contemporary Issues for 2002

Global Economics:
Contemporary Issues for 2002

David Begg

Global Economics : Contemporary Issues for 2002

David Begg

ISBN 0077099613

 Education

Published by McGraw-Hill Education
Shoppenhangers Road
Maidenhead
Berkshire
SL6 2QL
Telephone: 44 (0) 1628 502 500
Fax: 44 (0) 1628 770 224
Website: www.mcgraw-hill.co.uk

British Library Cataloguing in Publication Data

A catalogue record for this book is available from the British Library

Library of Congress Cataloguing in Publication Data

The Library of Congress data for this book has been applied for

Acquisitions Editor: Julian Partridge
Senior Development Editor: Caroline Howell
Editorial Assistant: Nicola Wimpory
Senior Marketing Manager: Petra Skytte
Senior Production Editorial Manager: Max Elvey
Acquisitions Editor, E-Learning: Roger Domingo
New Media Designer/Developer: Douglas Greenwood
Production Assistant: Alex Lawler

Produced for McGraw-Hill by Gecko Limited
Text design by Gecko Limited
Cover design by Gecko Limited
Printed and bound in Spain by Mateu Cromo

Acknowledgements

The publishers would like to thank the following individuals, institutions and companies for
permission to reproduce images in this book. Every effort has been made to trace ownership
of copyright. The publishers would be happy to make arrangements with any copyright
holder whom it has not been possible to contact.

Cover: DigitalVision; Airbus Industrie; Corbis, The Stock Market.

Airbus Industrie (64); Bundesbank (45); Corbis UK Ltd (9,11,25,37,42 right,46); European
Central Bank (9); Gecko Ltd (1,3,4,10,24,36,44); Image Bank (52); IMF (17 bottom,18 top,
19 top,19 bottom,20 bottom,58 right,59 bottom right); Popperfoto (20 bottom,58 right,
59 bottom right); PA News Photos (17 top,20 top,21 bottom,26,27,28,31 top,33,35,37,57
top,57 bottom,59 top,59 left,60,61 bottom); Topham Picturepoint (21 top,42 left,58 left,
59 bottom left); US Treasury (18 bottom); World Bank (2); www.amazon.com (23);
www.nasdaq.com (23); www.yahoo!.com (23).

Contents

Preface

New editions of our textbooks usually appear every three years, but the world does not stand still in between editions. This *Postscript* has been specially written by David Begg to update readers of both the sixth edition of Begg, Fischer and Dornbusch, *Economics*, published in 2000, and of its new sibling, *Foundations of Economics*, first published in 2001.

This *Postscript* deals with a range of topical issues—the health of the G7 economies, the collapse of the dot.com bubble, the recent fuel crisis, how the euro is doing and whether asylum seekers impose an economic burden. It also gives details of recent winners of the Nobel Prize for Economic Science, and discusses what contributions they made.

Economics is not a dead language but a lens through which we can watch our live and changing world. Enjoy the view.

Postscript Some interesting things have happened since the last edition was written. We use these margin notes to define key terms and summarize important ideas.

Test Quiz

Before you even look at this book, try the quiz below. The questions cover some of the issues economics think about.

1   Economics is the study of:

   a   how to produce the most goods for the most people;

   b   how society decides what, how, and for whom to produce;

   c   how to avoid waste and inefficiency.

2   a   By encouraging customers, lower food prices raise revenues of farmers.

   b   By discouraging customers, higher oil prices reduce revenues to oil producers.

   c   Neither of the above.

3   a   Higher income tax rates are a disincentive to work.

   b   Higher income tax rates are an incentive to work.

   c   Income tax rates have only a small effect on the incentive to work.

4   Public goods are:

   a   those provided by the public sector;

   b   those government believes people should consume;

   c   those which everyone must consume in the same quantity.

5   An increase in the proportion of income saved:

   a   tends to increase output since investment rises;

   b   tends to reduce output since consumer spending falls;

   c   tends to increase inflation since the money supply rises.

6   a   Inflation makes people worse off because goods become more expensive.

   b   Inflation makes a country uncompetitive in international markets.

   c   A high but constant rate of inflation need not be a major problem.

7 An exchange rate devaluation improves a country's international competitiveness:

    a   only after a few years;

    b   only for a few years;

    c   only if interest rates are simultaneously reduced.

8 It is well known that economics cannot forecast changes in stock market prices. This shows:

    a   that economics works;

    b   that economics pays insufficient attention to real world problems;

    c   neither of the above.

1 How healthy are the G7 countries?

The Group of Seven or G7 consists of the major advanced economies of the world: the United States, Japan, Germany, France, the UK, Italy and Canada. When Russia is also included, it becomes the G8. Political leaders of these countries have regular summit meetings to discuss economic issues of mutual interest. The civil servants who do most of the work preparing these meetings are known affectionately as sherpas (an admiring reference to the local mountaineers who guided climbers to the summits of the Himalayas).

These summit meetings are now famous as riot opportunities for those protesting against capitalism and globalization. Riots focus attention on the impact of the global economy on the poor and the disadvantaged. Among the demands of the protesters are more extensive debt relief for Heavily Indebted Poor Countries (HIPC) and the relaxation of patent laws to allow poor AIDS-afflicted countries access to anti-AIDS drugs at cheaper prices.

G7 The Group of Seven, the big economies: United States, Japan, Germany, France, UK, Italy and Canada.

G8 The Group of Eight: the G7 plus Russia.

Debt relief Consent by lenders to defer or write off debts of poor countries.

HIPC Heavily Indebted Poor Countries.

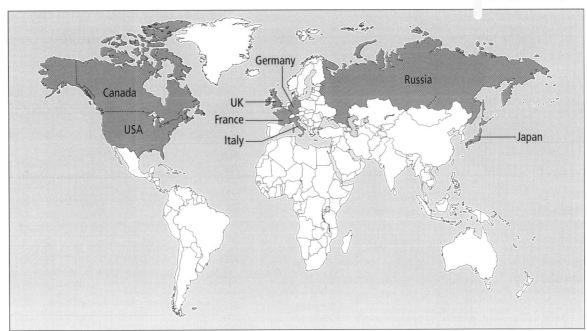

World map showing the location of all the G8 countries

IMF International Monetary Fund. Funded by member countries in proportion to GDP (Gross Domestic Product–a country's national output), the IMF lends and advises governments in economic trouble.

World Bank Funded by member countries in proportion to GDP, the World Bank lends at reasonable interest rates to finance investment in poor countries.

Internet A means of electronic communication and data transmission. The dot.com companies boomed until 2000, but many have since gone bankrupt. Section 2 gives details and discusses why.

Slow progress is being made on both issues. For example, the HIPC initiative, launched by the IMF and the World Bank in 1996 to provide a framework for lowering the debt burden in highly indebted poor countries, has been reinforced by programmes to support poverty reduction and improve social conditions. Some of the poorest African countries have now had over half of their debt written off, allowing more of their income to be spent on social programmes and investment in a better future. During 1990–2015 the aim is to halve the number of people in the world living in extreme poverty. Rich countries contribute directly and also indirectly, as the major contributors to the IMF and the World Bank. Critics say much more could be done.

Both domestic charities and international aid agencies are well aware that the attitude of donors can be affected by the state of donor economies. Rich countries in temporary economic difficulty may look for opportunities to be less generous. Moreover, slower growth in the G7 reduces the demand for exports from developing countries. The current health of the G7 economies is of significance not merely for those in rich countries but also for the poor of the world.

The World Bank, situated in Washington

Recent developments in the G7: the boom to mid-2000

Table 1-1 provides a recent snapshot of the G7 economies, giving data on real output growth and inflation in each country.

In the late 1990s the world economy enjoyed a boom, led by extremely rapid growth in North America. The internet revolution was in full swing and optimism was high. It seemed that

Table 1-1 G7 macroeconomic performance, 1998–2001 (%)

	UK	Germany	France	Italy	USA	Japan	Canada
Real growth							
1998	2.6	2.1	3.2	1.5	4.4	−2.5	3.3
1999	2.3	1.6	3.2	1.6	4.2	0.8	4.5
2000	3.0	3.0	3.2	2.9	5.0	1.7	4.7
2001	2.6	1.9	2.6	2.0	1.5	0.6	2.3
Inflation							
1998	2.4	1.1	0.7	2.2	1.1	0.2	1.0
1999	2.5	0.9	0.3	1.5	1.5	−0.9	1.6
2000	2.0	0.0	0.9	1.8	2.1	−1.5	3.3
2001	2.5	1.0	1.7	2.2	2.2	−0.4	2.4

Sources: OECD *Economic Outlook*, December 2000; IMF *World Economic Outlook*, May 2001.
Note: 2001 data are forecasts as of May 2001.

OECD The Organization for Economic Co-operation and Development, based in Paris, is a club of developed countries (currently 30) that meets to discuss issues of mutual concern.

OECD Economic Outlook, published twice a year, is a good place to keep track of what is going on.

productivity would grow rapidly for many years. Demand and output could safely be allowed to expand to match. Businesses were investing heavily in new technology, and households watched the value of their stock market holdings soar.

Map showing the poorest countries of the world

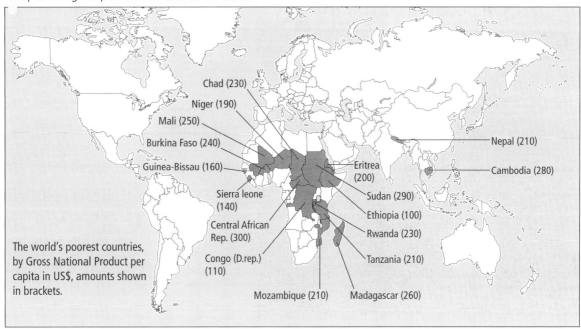

The world's poorest countries, by Gross National Product per capita in US$, amounts shown in brackets.

Chad (230)
Niger (190)
Mali (250)
Burkina Faso (240)
Guinea-Bissau (160)
Sierra leone (140)
Central African Rep. (300)
Congo (D.rep.) (110)
Mozambique (210)
Eritrea (200)
Sudan (290)
Ethiopia (100)
Rwanda (230)
Tanzania (210)
Madagascar (260)
Nepal (210)
Cambodia (280)

Eurozone Eleven EU countries formed a monetary union in January 1999. Greece has joined since. Members have permanently fixed exchange rates and a single interest rate.

A single currency, the euro, will begin circulating in 2002. We discuss the early years of the euro in Section 4.

Collateral Assets that borrowers pledge as security for a loan. Property market crashes often cause problems with collateral. Remember those UK householders with 'negative equity' in the early 1990s? The value of their houses had fallen below the value of their mortgages.

Some developments elsewhere in the world reinforced this trend. Asia bounced back rapidly from the crisis of 1997–98. Within Europe, the UK had grown steadily after its exit from the exchange rate mechanism in 1992. The countries of the eurozone had also bounced back from the Maastricht years, during which they tightened fiscal policy to confirm their fitness as initial candidates for the monetary union that began in 1999. Moreover, convergence on low inflation had meant that interest rates fell in countries where previously they had been high; and the perception that a single currency would help consolidate a single market within the eurozone boosted business and consumer confidence.

Only Japan was a source of concern. After the end of a property boom in the early 1990s, confidence in Japan collapsed. Banks had made loans taking property as collateral. Not only could borrowers not repay, but also the value of the collateral had fallen. The Japanese were reluctant to acknowledge, and therefore to deal with, the root cause of their problem, the insolvency of their banks. Thus the crisis lingered throughout the 1990s. Japan's output growth has been extremely low for a long time. However,

Map showing the OECD countries

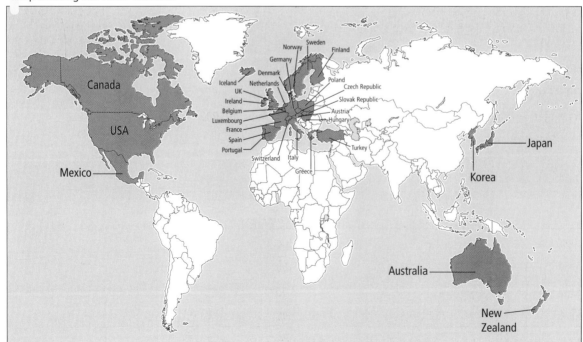

until 2000 Japan was the exception within the G7. Elsewhere, things were booming. The global economy could survive slow growth in its second largest economy because other countries were acting as locomotives of growth. Furthermore, strong demand for Japanese exports, particularly in North America, was mitigating the extent of the Japanese crisis.

After 2000 things changed rapidly. The American locomotive hit the buffers, and the rest of the train skidded towards a halt. Throughout 2001, forecasts of future growth were downgraded every month. Between October 2000 and May 2001, the IMF *World Economic Outlook* reduced its forecast of global growth during 2001 by 1 percentage point. Its next forecast will be lower still. Moreover, since it takes time to establish reliable data, even estimates of the recent past are becoming more pessimistic.

Why the bubble burst

Although European growth was never fast, growth rates in the United States and parts of Asia had been extremely rapid in 1999–2000. Some slowdown had been anticipated, not least because monetary policy had been deliberately tightened to prevent inflation picking up. Since monetary policy takes up to two years to have its full effect, it is always hard for policymakers to judge in advance quite how hard to apply the brakes.

Superimposed on monetary tightening, three new shocks occurred in 2000. The first was a sharp rise in oil prices. After years of weakness, OPEC got its act together again. Table 1-2 shows the surge of oil prices in 2000. These

> Since data take time to produce, the hardest task for economic forecasters is often to figure out where the economy is today.

> **Monetary policy** The use of interest rates to keep demand and spending roughly in line with the capacity to produce. Hence it is a policy to try to achieve price stability by preventing supply and demand getting out of line.

> **OPEC** The Organization of Petroleum Exporting Countries, responsible for 40 per cent of world oil production. We discuss OPEC in Section 3.

Table 1-2   Two clues: oil prices and the stock market, 1998–2001

	Oil price ($/barrel)	Share prices (NASDAQ index)
1998	12.6	1800
1999	17.3	2400
2000	28.3	4000
2001	25.5	1600

Note: Oil prices are annual averages; stock market data as at end July each year.

Oil production

data are annual averages; weekly data are even more dramatic. Oil prices increased from around $8 a barrel at the trough in 1998 to over $30 a barrel at the peak in 2000. We discuss how this led to a fuel crisis in Section 3.

Supply shock A change in the capacity shock to make output. Adverse shocks, by cutting supply relative to demand, cause price increases.

Oil price increases, like other adverse supply shocks, reduce output and increase inflation. Even at $30 a barrel, in real terms oil prices were not nearly as high in 2000 as when they previously reached $30 a barrel in 1980. Because of general inflation since 1980, oil prices would have to rise to $80 a barrel today to be equivalent in real terms to their 1980 value. The damaging effects of high real oil prices in the 1980s have not yet been repeated. This time round, the problem is much less severe. Nevertheless, oil prices did triple in only a couple of years during 1998–2000 and have remained quite high ever since. This was bound to have an adverse effect.

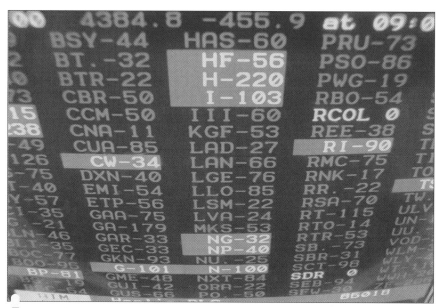

The most famous index in the UK is the 'Footsie', the FTSE index compiled by the *Financial Times* (FT) and Stock Exchange (SE).

The second major shock was the end of the optimism about rapid growth in future earnings of 'new-economy' stocks, particularly those in telecoms, the media and technology. Many internet share prices fell 90 per cent from their peak in 2000. Of course, one reason they could fall so much was that previously they had risen so much. Table 1-2 shows the behaviour of the NASDAQ, an index of share prices on a US stock exchange that specialises in high-tech and new-economy companies. Even this broad-based index has fallen by around 60 per cent. We discuss this further in Section 2.

How could people have been so wrong? Share prices reflect guesses about the entire

There were numerous casualties of the recent fall in .com share prices stream of dividends that a company will earn over its future lifetime. When internet companies began, from tiny bases, their initial growth was extremely rapid. Nobody knew whether this would be sustained or not. To start with, people assumed it would. At the first sign of slower growth, extrapolations of future growth changed significantly.

People changed their minds not merely about the size of these companies but also about their profitability. Monopolists make fat and sustained profits only when they can prevent imitators muscling in on the action. But internet start-ups are easy. Moreover, much of the capital of a successful high-tech firm resides in the brains of its staff, who can always jump ship or start their own company. So competition was more intense than first recognized; even firms with good ideas could not always rely on sustaining profits for a long time. Without the prospect of sustained profits, it is difficult to justify high share prices.

Once the United States sneezed, everyone else caught cold. The booming economies of Asia—often exporters of high-tech components to the US market—found their export markets drying up. Europeans found it harder to export to both the United States and Asia. In Japan, fragile confidence was quickly shattered again. With each new piece of bad news, talk of a rosy 2001 turned increasingly to talk of how to avoid outright recession.

Monetary policy to the rescue?

One of the principal institutional and political developments of the 1990s had been greater operational independence of central banks in setting interest rates. This reflected recognition that inflation had often been caused by lax policies pursued by politicians. If tough measures needed to be taken, this was more likely to be done by independent central bankers than by politicians who were dependent on public opinion.

Different countries pursued this new orthodoxy in slightly different ways. Central banks were rarely responsible for setting their own objectives; rather they were responsible for attaining objectives laid down by the constitution (as with the European Central Bank) or by the government (as with the Bank of England, whose inflation target is set by the Chancellor of the Exchequer). Although all central banks are responsible for attaining targets emphasizing price stability (often in practice defined as around 2–2.5 per cent inflation), they vary in the extent to which they are also expected to pay some attention to output fluctuations over the business cycle. Whatever the minor variations across countries, operational independence for central banks has to date been a great success. High inflation in the 1970s and 1980s was replaced by low inflation in the 1990s (see Table 1-1).

How did monetary policy cope with the boom of the late 1990s and the sharp slowdown in 2001? Figure 1-1, on the following page, shows the evolution of interest rates in the United States, the UK and the eurozone. All three central banks were forced to raise interest rates after mid-1999, as the combination of the oil price shock and a booming world economy threatened to lead to a new bout of inflation. Since this danger was greatest in the United States, which was overheating the most, the increases in interest rates were also largest there. The new European Central Bank (ECB), keen to establish a track record of being tough on inflation, also raised interest rates steadily.

Note the distinction between large and small economies. Large economies trade a lot internally; exports and imports are a small share of their GDP. Small economies have to specialize to be competitive, and hence have high exports and imports in relation to GDP. Small economies are more sensitive to the exchange rate. One reason the Bank of England raised interest rates less than central banks in the United States or the eurozone after mid-1999 was that the high level of the sterling exchange rate was already making UK exports uncompetitive, thus putting a brake on the level of economic activity.

High interest rates These cool down the economy by reducing spending by firms and households.

ECB The European Central Bank, based in Frankfurt, sets interest rates in the eurozone.

Openness This is measured by the share of exports or imports in a country's GDP. Small countries are usually open. A large country like the United States trades mainly with itself and is much less open.

The Bank of England

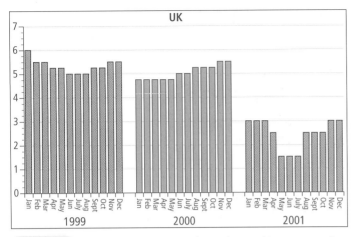

Figure 1-1   This graph demonstrates the evolution of interest rates in the United States, the UK and the eurozone between 1999 and 2001.

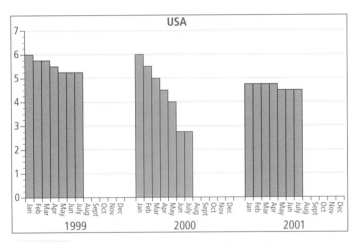

Figure 1-1   This graph demonstrates the evolution of interest rates in the United States, the UK and the eurozone between 1999 and 2001.

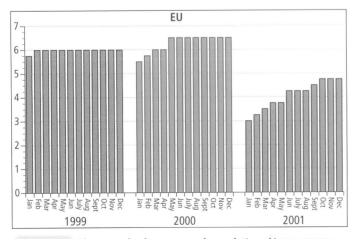

Figure 1-1   These graphs demonstrate the evolution of interest rates in the United States, the UK and the eurozone between 1999 and 2001.

The steady rise in interest rates until the end of 2000 shows that central bankers were mainly preoccupied with staving off inflation. However, when the turnaround came, it quickly snowballed. Central banks were therefore faced with a need to worry about slowing output growth, despite the fact that, because higher oil prices were still feeding through into output prices, inflation was temporarily near or above the target rate that central banks were supposed to achieve.

This was not an easy situation in which to set interest rates. The more confident a central bank was that its inflation-fighting credentials were already soundly established, the more it would be expected to ignore the blip in oil prices (which were likely to fall again if the world economy was slowing down) and cut interest rates to soften the fall in output. Conversely, a central bank still under scrutiny might have to pay more attention to fighting inflation, especially if its mandate appeared to place a lower emphasis on the need to mitigate output fluctuations over the business cycle.

Inflation dynamics
Current inflation is still being affected by things that happened in the past two years, as changes in input prices gradually feed through into output prices. Changes in interest rates therefore take up to two years to have their full effect on inflation and output.

Business cycle
Fluctuations in output around its long-run trend.

The Federal Reserve Bank in the United States of America

Figure 1-1 confirms the relevance of this reasoning in practice. In the United States, the Federal Reserve acted repeatedly to cut interest rates in 2001, progressively easing monetary policy as the extent of the slowdown became evident. The Bank of England did the same, although less vigorously. In contrast, the European Central Bank was reluctant to cut interest rates while inflation remained around 3 per cent.

So what next?

By the time you read this you may know the answer! Nevertheless, it is interesting to see where the economic logic leads us. The IMF *World Economic Outlook* published in May 2001 identified a number of reasons the slowdown might be comparatively moderate and short-lived:

- Cuts in interest rates take time to have their full effect.

- The slowdown will cut the demand for oil, reduce oil prices and inflation, and allow more scope for 'non-inflationary' interest rate cuts.

- Interest rates are generally around 4–5 per cent and hence can be reduced further if necessary.

- Even if monetary policy fails to avert recession, looser fiscal policy will still be a stimulus. Both the eurozone and the United States are currently easing fiscal policy.

UK monetary policy
The Bank of England has kept inflation low, but it has also been more willing than the ECB to cut interest rates to avoid recession.

Fiscal policy The use of government budgetary policy to affect the balance of supply and demand in the economy.

John Maynard Keynes
(1883–1946)

These arguments offer some comfort, but they are no guarantee that policy can offset any further bad news that may occur. In countries like the United States, fiscal changes take time because Congress and the president must agree. Even after policy is changed, it takes time for business and consumers to respond. Moreover, greater dissaving by the government may induce greater saving by the private sector—people may recognize that today's budget deficit adds to tomorrow's debt interest, which the government will have to finance by higher future taxes. If people see higher taxes looming, they may start saving in advance in order to be able to pay.

The consensus of economists is that, in normal times, monetary and fiscal policy are both useful weapons in moderating fluctuations in output. The best reason to use these weapons may be to ensure that times stay normal. To remind us how policy can lose its power, we need only look again at Japan.

Pushing on a string

The economist John Maynard Keynes once compared monetary policy to a string. Pulling on a string always has the desired effect, but pushing on a string may lead simply to a loose string. Higher interest rates are likely to reduce aggregate demand for goods and services, but lower interest rates have less predictable effects. In normal times they boost demand, but sometimes they have no effect. For example, if businesses expect to make operating losses, they may stop investing however low the interest rate is. This special circumstance in which monetary expansion becomes powerless is known as the liquidity trap.

In the Great Depression of the 1930s, economists argued about whether the liquidity trap was relevant. Keynes believed that it was. Moreover, if monetary policy had become powerless only fiscal expansion could restore full employment. The arms race prior to the Second World War was certainly operated in this direction.

Post-war economists quickly forgot the liquidity trap, which then disappeared from textbooks. Economies close to full employment operated in the normal range, in which lower interest rates clearly boosted demand and spending. However, recent Japanese experience is leading to the reintroduction of the liquidity trap into textbooks. With stagnation in the Japanese economy (apart from 1996, since 1991 output has not grown by more than 2 per cent in any year), the Bank of Japan tried easing monetary policy. Interest rates have been under 1 per cent since 1996, and now are almost zero. They cannot go lower. Yet still people refuse to spend.

Going back to Table 1-1, the problems in Japan got so bad that the country started to experience deflation. Prices actually fell. Everyone remembers that inflation was a great problem in the 1970s and 1980s throughout the OECD. You may think that if inflation is bad, deflation or negative inflation can be good. This is not so. When people see prices falling, they postpone spending in the expectation that they can buy more cheaply later. Spending dries up, demand falls and deflation intensifies. Moreover, debts denominated in nominal or money values become more onerous to repay as prices and nominal incomes fall. Bankruptcies increase, and the banking system comes under further pressure. Even with zero nominal interest rates, falling prices mean that real interest rates are positive. If deflation is large enough, in terms of real interest rates monetary policy must be quite tight.

Stagnation Slow or negative output growth. When this is combined with high inflation, it is called stagflation.

Deflation Falling prices, or negative inflation.

Real interest rates The actual or nominal interest rate minus the inflation rate during the same period; hence the extra quantity of goods a lender can get by deferring spending.

Budget deficit An excess of government spending over revenue. Such deficits add to the debt of the government.

There is always fiscal policy

If monetary policy has not worked, there is always fiscal policy on which to fall back. Normally, we say that fiscal expansion boosts demand. Even though people realize that a budget deficit increases government debt, and hence future

Armament manufacturing in the Second World War

Just a few of the luxury items which suffer when deflation occurs

taxes to pay the higher interest payments, people compensate only partially by raising saving today in order to be able to afford these future tax increases. Fiscal policy works in normal times.

Why might looser fiscal policy fail to boost demand? Suppose the government announces an emergency fiscal expansion because the economy is stagnating and monetary policy is not working. People may conclude that the government is doing this only because its forecast of the future is even more bleak than the general public had realized. If things are really this bad, it makes sense to spend even less. Fiscal expansion then fails to boost demand. Moreover, a succession of failed fiscal expansions adds so much to government debt that people then begin to anticipate seriously high taxes in future in order to finance the government's payments of interest on the debt.

Expectations matter
Private spending by firms and households depends not just on how well they are doing today, but also on how well they expect to be doing in the future. Anything that depresses these expectations may make people spend less today.

Table 1-3 Japan's macroeconomic misery, 1993–2001

	GDP growth (%)	Interest rate (%)	Budget deficit (% of GDP)	Government net debt (% of GDP)
1993	0	3	2	5
1994	1	2	2	8
1995	2	1	4	13
1996	5	1	4	16
1997	1	1	3	18
1998	−3	1	5	31
1999	0	0	7	38
2000	2	0	6	44
2001	2	0	6	49

Source: OECD *Economic Outlook*, December 2000.

Possible in theory but not in practice? Alas, no. Table 1-3 documents the macroeconomic misery of Japan since 1992: stagnating output, the failure of low interest rates, the increasing resort to budget deficits and the consequent rapid debt build-up. The G7 will never be fully healthy until Japan recovers. So far, the extraordinary health of the United States has covered up the impact of the sickness in Japan. If the United States now falters, the world economy is unlikely to prosper when its two largest countries are in trouble.

As noted earlier, much of the source of Japan's woes was the evaporation of confidence in the soundness of its banking system. Until this is fixed, altering the macroeconomic policy pedals may continue to fail. International agencies continue to recommend structural change, greater transparency, better financial supervision and greater competition.

After this initial look at the G7, we look in more detail at the key shocks identified above, the collapse of stock market confidence, particularly in the new-economy stocks, and the dramatic rise in oil prices after 1998.

Useful websites For material in this section see:
www.imf.org
www.oecd.org
www.bankofengland.co.uk
www.ecb.int
www.federalreserve.gov
www.boj.or.jp

Further reading For a full treatment, read:
Begg, Fischer, Dornbusch: *Economics, 6/e*, McGraw-Hill, 2000
Chapter 25 (monetary & fiscal)
Chapter 26 (supply shocks)
Chapter 28 (inflation)
Chapter 31 (business cycles)

Alternatively, for a streamlined introduction, read:
Begg, Fischer, Dornbusch: *Foundations of Economics*, McGraw-Hill, 2001
Chapter 8-3 (money & output)
Chapter 9-3 (inflation)
Chapter 11-2 (business cycles)

Some influential figures in the G8

Alan Greenspan became the US Federal Reserve Chairman in 1988 and has been renominated ever since. Greenspan is the most powerful unelected official in Washington and guides the US economy. Born in 1926 in New York City, Greenspan studied at the Juilliard School of Music and played in Jerome's swing band. He went on to study economics, completing his PhD at New York University. He does most of his work, including the writing of speeches and testimonies, in the bath. Greenspan has a wry sense of humour, enjoys reading early Clive Cussler mysteries, and prefers mashed potatoes to nouvelle cuisine.

Gordon Brown, the UK Chancellor of the Exchequer, is a key figure not just in the UK Labour government but on the world stage. He currently chairs the IMF's International Monetary and Financial Committee. Born in Glasgow in 1951, Brown has a doctorate in history and lectured in politics before becoming current affairs editor of Scottish Television. Elected to Parliament for Dunfermline East, in opposition he shadowed Trade and Industry and the Treasury until Labour's election victory in 1997. A student activist in the 1970s, and author of many books, his interests include football, tennis and films. He and his wife Sarah Macauley are expecting their first child.

Hans Eichel has been a member of the Socialist SPD party since 1964 and was appointed as Germany's Minister of Finance in April 2000. Born in 1941, Eichel studied philosophy, political science, education and history at the University of Berlin and, having trained as a teacher, became vice-principal of a high school. Between 1975 and 1991, Eichel was mayor of his hometown of Kassel. He then served as premier of Hesse until 1999. Eichel is married with two children and enjoys taking his summer breaks at Langeoog by the North Sea.

Paul H. O'Neill was sworn in as US Secretary of the Treasury in January 2001. Born in 1935 in St Louis, Missouri, he completed his economics degree and Masters in Public Administration, and became an engineer and then a computer system analyst. At Ford he rose to deputy director of the office of management and budget. He served as director of Aluminium Alcoa Inc., and transformed this old-economy firm into a new-economy success. As head of a major corporation with 140 000 employees in 36 countries, O'Neill gained insights into international finance and the global economy. O'Neill enjoys painting in watercolours and is a good friend of Alan Greenspan.

Laurent Fabius was appointed as France's Minister of Economics, Finance and Industry in March 2000. Born in 1946, Fabius joined the Socialist Party in 1974. He was elected Prime Minister under Mitterrand in July 1984, but was deposed two years later. He was then active as an MEP between 1989 and 1992, lost the Socialist Party leadership to Jospin in 1990 and has been mayor of Grand Quevilly since 1995. He was elected as President of the National Assembly in June 1997 and has chaired numerous political committees. Fabius is the author of four political books, one of which won a national award. He is married with two children and enjoys horse riding.

Paul Martin was sworn in as Canada's Minister of Finance in November 1993, and was re-appointed in 1997. Born in Windsor, Ontario, in 1938, he studied philosophy, attended law school, then became a member of Parliament in 1988. His experience has primarily been gained in the private sector, as chairman and chief executive officer of Canada Steamship Lines and as corporate director for seven major Canadian companies. In September 1999, Martin was named inaugural chair of the G-20. Martin is married with three sons and works with a wide range of community and service organizations.

Masajuro Shiokawa, a 79-year-old veteran lawmaker who sides with the Mori faction of the Liberal LDP, was appointed as Japan's Minister of Finance in spring 2001. Shiokawa's political career has been diverse: Minister of Transport, Minister of Home Affairs and Minister of Education, and Cabinet Secretary twice. He has admitted that he is not an expert in economics, having completed a degree in this field some 57 years ago. However, his debut at the G8 meeting demonstrated that he is a fast learner. Affectionately known as 'Shio-san' by the younger members of his party faction, colleagues find a tough man under the affable exterior.

Giulio Tremonti, Italy's Minister of Economics and Finance, assumed office in June 2001 as a member of the centre-right Forza Italia government. Born 1947 in Sondrio, Tremonti studied law and became a law professor before founding his own law firm in 1986. As member of the Patto Segni party in 1994, Tremonti held the post of Minister of Economics and Finance and President of the Commission for Monetary Reform in the first Berlusconi government. During this time, Tremonti made a name as a lawgiver, passing a law bearing his name that provided tax cuts for reinvested profits. Tremonti is the author of many books on tax and public policy and is editor of a financial magazine.

Aleksey Leonidovich Kudrin was appointed as Russia's Finance Minister and Deputy Premier in May 2000. Born in Dobel, Latvia, in 1960, Kudrin completed an economics degree at Leningrad State University in 1983 and began his career in academia. He later became deputy mayor of St Petersburg and, in 1990, president of the city's Administration Committee for Economics and Finance. Kudrin is married with two young children. He enjoys sport, reading Tolstoy and listening to classical and jazz music. He used to play the drums in a rock band.

Pedro Solbes Mira became the European Commissioner for Economic and Financial Affairs in 1999. Born in 1942 in Pinoso, Spain, Solbes took a degree in law and then a doctorate in political sciences at Madrid University. Since the early 1970s, Solbes's work has centred on the European Community. Solbes chaired the joint committee of the Spanish Parliament on the European Union in 1996. Previously, he was Director General for Commercial Policy at the Ministry of Economics and Commerce, Minister of Agriculture, Fisheries and Food, and Minister for Economics and Finance.

2 The dot.com massacre

Some students have conservative views and like reading *The Times*. Others hate its politics but like its crossword. Both get to read acerbic columns on economics by Anatole Kaletsky. Every January, Kaletsky makes predictions for the coming year. In January 2000, at the height of the stock market boom in internet companies, he bravely forecast that their share prices would be halved within a year. It turned out to be an underestimate of the fall.

Within ten months he was reporting on the carnage:

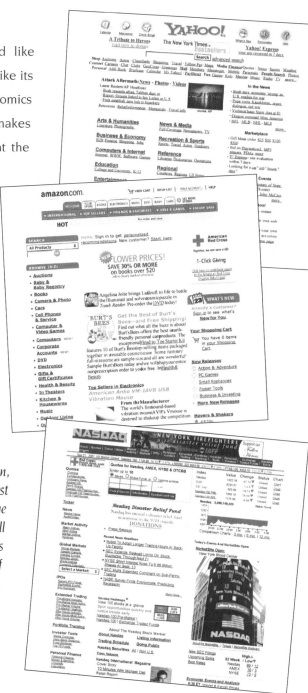

> *I was driving around San Francisco and found my way blocked by a delivery truck from Webvan.com. I recalled that this online delivery company was expected last year to become the biggest food business in America, but was soon forced to cut back its operations to just a few towns…. Another sure-fire winner was stamps.com, a company briefly worth almost $1 billion, after acquiring a supposedly priceless asset, the first licence from the American Government to sell postage stamps online…. It is becoming apparent that all Internet companies, including even the giants, are as grotesquely overvalued as were the industrial giants of Japan in the bubble economy of 1989. If this is true, then the massacre of Internet and technology firms has hardly even begun. This may be hard to believe for investors in companies such as Yahoo! who have already suffered losses of 70 per cent from this year's peak, Amazon.com (down 75 per cent), or even Microsoft (down 55 per cent).*

(*The Times*, 20 October 2000)

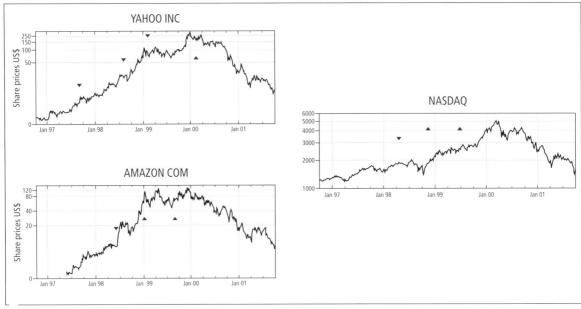

The internet bubble
bursts

He was right again. Since October 2000, these new-economy stocks have taken a further battering. The three graphs show the rise and fall of the share prices of online giants Amazon and Yahoo! on the NASDAQ index of high-tech stocks.

All three charts have a logarithmic scale on the vertical axis, meaning that a given vertical distance shows a percentage change, not an absolute change. For example, Yahoo!'s share price had fallen from a peak of around $220 to a low of $11, a decrease of 95 per cent. In the courtroom-addicted United States, people are now suing investment banks whose so-called experts advised people to invest in these stocks just before they collapsed. Why couldn't people see it coming?

Asset price bubbles

Asset prices These may obey the fundamentals implied by demand and cost in that industry, or may follow a speculative bubble.

Suppose the 'right' price of a share is £10. This price is justified by the 'fundamentals' of the company, or sensible projections of its future performance. Suppose everybody agrees what these are, and everybody agrees what the right price is. One equilibrium is that the price is £10. But, disturbingly, there are other equilibria.

Could £11 be an equilibrium for the share price today? Anything other than £10 is called a bubble, a departure from the fundamentals. Suppose the market thinks there is a 50 per cent chance the bubble will continue tomorrow, and a 50 per cent chance it will burst. If it bursts, the share reverts to its fundamentals-inspired price.

You are wondering whether or not to hold the share that is currently trading at £11. If the bubble bursts, you lose £1 because tomorrow the price will be £10. Suppose you think the price will go up to £12 if the bubble does not burst. Hence you have a 50 per cent chance of making £1 and a 50 per cent chance of losing £1. The market is offering you a fair bet. You are happy to hold the share at £11.

Bubble An acceleration of asset prices away from the price justified by a company's fundamentals; a temporary bandwagon that is a self-fulfilling prophecy.

Famous bubbles These include the South Sea Bubble, a speculative trading venture in which people like Sir Isaac Newton lost a fortune; and the Dutch Tulip mania, where people speculated on the price of bulbs of rare tulips.

A cartoon symbolising the South Sea Bubble and the ruin faced by many of its investors. Greed and suffering are symbolised, clergy gamling, satan bearing a scythe and people being literally 'taken for a ride' on a merry go round. *By J Moore after the cartoon by William Hogarth*

A trader signals his last trades just before trading closes

Speculator Someone who buys an asset in the hope of reselling later at a higher price.

Tomorrow arrives, and, as it happens, the bubble has not burst. The price is now £12. Should you keep holding the share? Now a bust means you lose £2 if the price reverts to £10. But you will still happily hold the share if you think that, provided the bubble continues, the price will be £14 tomorrow. You then have a 50–50 chance of winning or losing £2.

Maybe the bubble then bursts. If not, the next day the price stands at £14, and it takes the belief that it will rise to £18—a possible gain of £4 to offset the danger of a loss of £4—to keep you on the speculative bandwagon.

The key feature of asset price bubbles is therefore that the price must accelerate while the bubble lasts. Every extra day the price is dangerously further from the sane price implied by the fundamentals, and it takes the lure of an ever larger gain to offset this risk.

Eventually, of course, the bubble bursts. Precisely when is impossible to predict. But the bubble could last for some time. During this period, everyone is aware that a bubble is going on, but a clear financial calculation makes it rational to participate.

In the preceding example, a bubble could arise even though everyone agreed on the price implied by the fundamentals. An additional difficulty in the internet revolution was that estimates of the prices implied by fundamentals differed greatly. Would new business opportunities expand at 8 per cent a year, 12 per cent a year or 20 per cent a year? Extrapolations over the next 20 years yielded radically different answers depending on which growth rate was assumed, and past evidence was only vaguely relevant to making future guesstimates for this new technology.

The past two years have provided the first data with which to make better assessments. For example, we now know that take-up of the next generation of mobile phones, with full internet capability, has been slower than originally forecast. But it is not merely the quantities of activity that have now been reassessed. The greatest change of mind has been about the ability to earn revenue and hence make profits.

> Things look a little gloomy for the telecommunications companies that paid a total of £22.5 billion for UK third generation mobile telephone licences in April last year.
>
> (Financial Times, 28 March 2001)

The article went on to note:

> 'classical economics' dictates that licences are a 'sunk cost' which cannot be reclaimed.... If companies holding licences would not have colluded to push up prices before the auctions for licences had been dreamt up, so this argument goes, they will not do so afterwards.

Lone voices Not everyone was taken in by the dazzling heights reached by share prices. Robert Shiller, a Yale economics professor, wrote a bestseller entitled *Irrational Exuberance* warning of the crash to come.

Central bankers also worried—that is what they are paid for. Alan Greenspan, chairman of the US Fed, voiced his concerns out loud. So did European Central Bankers, such as Sir Eddie George of the Bank of England.

Central bankers are not always this clear. Greenspan is also famous for the remark: 'If you think you understood me, you misunderstood.'

Alan Greenspan, the US Federal Reserve Board Chairman

The *Financial Times* noted that fears of bankruptcy might make phone companies so desperate that they will find a way to behave like OPEC, getting together to collude to raise prices and inhibit competition. Whether or not they would get away with it depends partly on how watchful the telephone regulator turns out to be.

Mobile phones are an example where the new technology was profitable, but the government, by auctioning off the right to use the airwaves, managed to grab these profits for the taxpayer. Since the auction occurred at the peak of the optimism, with hindsight the phone companies bid too much. This is why their finances look a lot less rosy than they did a year ago.

In other cases, the bad news came not from the government appropriating the profits, but from the prospect of profits being competed away by new firms continually entering the same market. Everyone wanted to start their own Lastminute.com. As the market was flooded, and estimates of the length of the initial loss-making phase increased, the ability to survive often depended more on a firm's relations with its bankers than the soundness of its underlying idea.

Markets that can be exuberantly high can also overreact to the subsequent fall. By the time you read this, it is possible that pessimism about new-economy stocks will have begun to ebb again. But understanding the extent of the pessimism it engendered in 2000–01 is important to an appreciation of the shocks hitting the global economy during that period. The other major shock was the rise in oil prices, to which we now turn.

Useful websites For material in this section, and its continuing development, see the websites of the *Financial Times,* the *Economist,* the *Guardian,* the *Times,* or the *BBC*:
www.ft.com
www.economist.com
www.guardian.co.uk
www.thetimes.co.uk
www.bbc.co.uk

Further reading For a full treatment, read:
Begg, Fischer, Dornbusch: *Economics, 6/e*, McGraw-Hill, 2000
    Chapter 10 (imperfect competition)
    Chapter 11 (e-commerce))
    Chapter 19 (regulation)

Alternatively, for a streamlined introduction, read:
Begg, Fischer, Dornbusch: *Foundations of Economics*, McGraw-Hill, 2001
    Chapter 3-3 (imperfect competition)
    Chapter 3-4 (e-markets)
    Chapter 6-2 (regulation)

---

3 Who caused the fuel crisis? Did it need solving?

In September 2000, the UK was almost brought to a standstill by a blockade of wholesale oil supplies. Not in the Persian Gulf and not organized by trade unions, but as a result of a spontaneous protest—largely by lorry drivers and farmers, traditional heavy users of fuel—within the UK. They enjoyed huge public support. People minded that petrol and diesel prices had gone through the roof, and wanted government to 'fix' the problem.

Some people said this had been caused by a resurgence of OPEC, the world cartel of oil producers. Others said that it was the result of a deliberate attempt by government to raise taxes on fuel, either actively or as a result of their automatic connection to oil prices. People argued that fuel was unfairly taxed, and that results were also inefficient. Let's take a closer look at some of the issues.

Fuel prices at the pump These reflect not just the price of crude oil, but also the costs and profits of oil refiners and the taxes levied by government.

Cartel A group of producers jointly deciding about output and prices, usually trying to cut joint output to create scarcity and force up the price.

Fuel protesters meet up at Gateway service station on the M1 prior to joining fuel protesters from across Britain who are heading for London and the climax of their campaign for lower petrol and diesel taxes

Fuel protestors walk from their lorries, which had been parked on the A40 (M) Westway in central London, towards a rally in Hyde Park. The truckers hoped to persuade the Government to reduce tax on fuel

OPEC market share
When OPEC first raised oil prices in 1973, it created an incentive for other countries to try harder to find their own oil.

OPEC and the world oil market

The Organization of Petroleum Exporting Countries (OPEC) was founded in 1960 and currently has 11 members. Table 3-1 shows their share of world oil output. OPEC produces just under 40 per cent of world oil, perhaps less than you thought.

Why then is OPEC so significant? Because these countries are part of a cartel that tries to co-operate to set a common price and make common decisions on output levels. In 1973, OPEC first managed to agree a significant reduction in oil output. Since rich countries needed a lot of oil, whatever the price, in economic speak, their demand was extremely price inelastic. OPEC countries calculated correctly that by cutting their output they could make oil scarce and force the price up a lot. When the price tripled in 1973–74, OPEC countries grew rich, despite the fact that they were producing less.

Table 3-1 World oil production (major countries)

OPEC	%	Non OPEC	%
Saudi Arabia	12	USA	10
Iran	5	Russia	9
Iraq	4	Mexico	5
Venezuela	4	Canada	4
Nigeria	3	China	4
United Arab Emirates	3	Norway	4
Indonesia	2	UK	4
Libya	2	**Total**	**40**
Algeria	2		
Kuwait	1		
Qatar	1		
Total	**39**	**Other small producers**	**21**

In response to high oil prices, rich countries gradually figured out how to supply a bit more oil themselves and demand a bit less. In 1979–80, OPEC responded to weakening oil prices by a further round of output cuts, doubling the price again. By the early 1980s, oil prices were around $30–35 a barrel. But do not confuse this with the price of $30 in autumn 2000. The scarcity of oil is measured by its real, or inflation-adjusted, price. To be the equivalent in real terms of $30 a barrel in 1980, today's oil prices would have to be over $80 a barrel. Because there was a lot of inflation during 1980–2000, prices had to rise a lot merely to preserve their real, inflation-adjusted value.

Against this background, the fact that after 1982 oil prices fell steadily in nominal terms, and spent much of 1986–99 in the range $10–20 a barrel, shows just how much the real price had fallen after the early 1980s. Like most cartels, OPEC was unable to sustain joint cuts in output over a long

Oil workers drilling for oil in Saudi Arabia, known to have the worlds richest reserves

period. Once the price was high, each individual member wanted to expand, not to maintain the cut in production.

By 1999, the nominal price of oil had fallen to around $8 a barrel, perhaps only one-tenth of its real price two decades earlier. Since 1999, it has risen sharply, partly because the booming world economy had raised the demand for oil, and partly because after years of less effective action, OPEC has been rejuvenated as a cohesive organization capable (but for how long?) of agreeing cuts in output in order to force up the price. Thus oil prices rose from around $8 in 1998 to over $30 a barrel in 1999–2000. The rich countries tried to convince OPEC that any price above $25 was likely to do so much damage in rich countries that demand for oil, and hence the price OPEC can charge for an extended period, was likely to fall sharply.

By 2001, the world economy was clearly slowing down. Higher oil prices were one of the causes; the bursting of the enthusiastic internet bubble was another. Whatever the cause of the slowdown, the consequence for oil prices was clear. As demand decreased, oil prices slipped to under $25 a barrel by mid-2001.

There are many good websites addressing these issues. You can look at OPEC's own site (www.opec.org). Even more useful is the extensive online material at BBC Online (www.bbc.co.uk/news/world/opec).

So higher petrol prices arose because OPEC managed to restrict supply?

Yes, especially in the short run, but that was far from the whole story. First, given a booming world economy in the late 1990s, oil companies took the opportunity to increase their profit margins. Oil companies reported large profits, especially in 2000. Some of the rise in domestic oil prices was not the result of OPEC supply but of higher global demand before 2001. Firms generally have higher profit margins during booms and lower margins in slumps.

Another important issue was taxes. Some taxes (such as VAT) are a constant percentage of the untaxed price. So when raw material prices rise, the absolute value of the tax increases (although it remains a constant share of the final tax-inclusive price). This effect alone meant that European governments obtained significant extra tax revenue as oil prices rose without having to change tax rates at all.

Furthermore, there has been a conscious policy in crowded, congested Europe of trying to discourage car use by deliberately taxing fuel so that users pay closer to the full social cost (including congestion and pollution) of using fuel to drive their cars. Throughout the 1990s, UK governments raised fuel duties faster than the rate of inflation to increase the price of car use. Note, though, that fuel taxes are not the only way this result can be achieved. In July 2001, Ken Livingstone, London's mayor, announced the introduction of a daily £5 congestion charge for people wishing to bring cars into central London.

Europeans care about these issues because Europe is congested. In contrast, in the uncongested land of the free and home of the brave, Americans pay much lower taxes on petrol. Many Americans assume that if cars had been around when the US constitution was first framed, Americans would have had a right to drive cars as well as a right to bear arms. To give some idea of the transatlantic discrepancy, fuel tax accounts for 22 per cent of the cost of petrol in the United States, compared with 72 per cent of the cost in the UK.

If both countries suffered equal congestion and pollution, it would be hard to make sense of such a large differential. However, the United States is land abundant, and much of Western Europe is densely populated, so the true burden of congestion and pollution in the latter is much larger. Some (significant) transatlantic difference

Fuel taxes These are intended to make fuel prices better reflect the congestion and pollution associated with fuel use.

Targeting Even if we decide to intervene to reduce pollution and congestion, we want policies to be targeted as accurately as possible on the problem, to minimize undesirable side effects. Some fuel uses do more damage than others. Fuel tax is quite a blunt instrument.

Externalities Direct physical spillovers through which one person's actions affect other people. Examples include pollution and congestion.

Ken Livingstone, Mayor of London

in fuel prices can therefore be justified. Whether the proper differential is as large (or larger) than the current amount is hard to calculate, even on pure efficiency grounds (making people pay for all the induced effects of what they do; what economists call internalising 'externalities' that spill over from one individual's actions on to another).

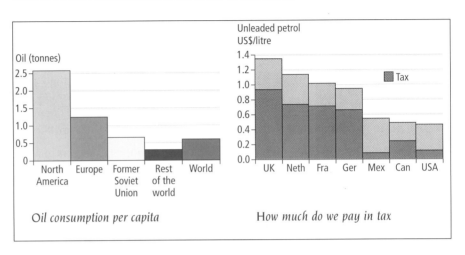

Oil consumption per capita

How much do we pay in tax

The left chart shows the very different taxation of unleaded petrol on the two sides of the Atlantic. The right chart shows that low taxes in North America do indeed induce users to respond by demanding more fuel. Economists believe that (appropriately) high taxes on fuel are part of a strategy for the proper pricing of environmental resources, and the only safe route to preserving our planet in the long run.

But poor people cannot afford to pay!

Who do you think has 3-litre cars that drink petrol? Not the poor. Even flat rate tax on petrol is quite progressive—not only do poor people pay less tax in absolute amounts, they also pay a smaller percentage of their income in fuel tax.

However, many of us would want to go further. The combined tax and social security system recognizes not merely that it is sometimes appropriate to take disproportionately from the rich, but that sometimes the poor need not just zero taxes but also subsidies. Many environmentalists who want to use the price mechanism argue in favour of a 'poll subsidy'.

Give everyone a flat rate handout, and then claw back the revenue from those previously paying too little for energy use by levying fuel duties that take account of the true social cost of using fuel. This way the poor as well as the environment can be protected. Economists regard this as distinguishing two different motives for taxation: to improve efficiency of resource use and to redistribute some spending power from richer to poorer people.

Politicians know only too well that issues about redistribution are usually much harder to resolve than issues about efficiency. Redistribution—the favouring of one group at the expense of another—automatically creates vocal losers who can make political trouble. Efficiency gains from better policies offer a pure surplus, which can be shared out among many people to assemble a majority for the policy. Of course, in the real world, most changes have consequences for both efficiency and distribution. We discussed earlier how policies explicitly targeted to help the poor could stop efficiency improvements from having adverse distribution consequences.

Summing up

After 1999, the UK Treasury benefited from additional taxation induced only by the rise in oil prices caused initially by two things: the world boom of the

Poll tax or poll subsidy
A flat tax or subsidy where everyone pays or gets the same, whatever their income or spending. Mrs Thatcher was forced from office partly because her poll tax was thought unfair. People wanted tax to reflect ability to pay, at least to some degree.

Efficiency Avoiding waste. However, an outcome can be efficient but unfair. People care about both.

The UK treasury

CAP The Common Agricultural Policy of the European Union. A system of price controls that is meant to smooth out fluctuations in food prices. The price paid to farmers has always been artificially high, leading to oversupply.

late 1990s and a reinvigorated OPEC. Should higher tax receipts have been used to help those most acutely affected by higher fuel duties, especially road hauliers? A responsible government must recognize the likely volatility of oil prices in the future. If it cuts taxes when oil prices rise, would it be prepared in the future to raise taxes every time oil prices fell? This is likely to be a political nightmare. Although the UK government made some concessions to the worst affected groups in 2000, it tried hard to avoid setting any precedents.

Moreover, it was well-meaning attempts to stabilize agricultural prices that gave Europe the Common Agricultural Policy (CAP) some 40 years ago. Policies of undue interest to one particular group quickly become the focus of their intense lobbying. They have a strong interest in manipulating the policy to their advantage. The rest of us, who have to finance it, have much less individual interest in it, since its burden is spread across so many of us. In the subsequent lobbying war, it is an unequal contest between the motivated and the apathetic. This explains the government's reluctance to acknowledge any regular linkage between world oil prices and levels of UK fuel taxation.

Lastly, there is the environmental impact. Politicians of all parties claim that the environment will be safe in their hands. Historically, pleading with the public has not proved a big success in limiting pollution and environmental damage. A tax on the activities that do the damage often seems like a tax without a benefit. It will not be popular, and hence politically attractive, until voters clearly understand how behaviour will change. High taxes have gradually reduced cigarette smoking, although better information has had a major effect. We need to tackle the environment as well, and we need to target measures as accurately as possible on the real problems.

Some environmental problems can be solved within a country; parking in London is an example. Other problems, such as global warming, have cross-border effects and need solutions that involve the co-operation of different governments. In turn, this raises issues about whether closer international integration is eroding the sovereignty of nation states.

Mention sovereignty to a Brit, and he or she automatically assumes you must be talking about the euro. Should the UK give up the pound? We do not have space for a full answer, but we can at least give a progress report on how the euro is doing.

Useful websites These include that of OPEC, an excellent study of the fuel crisis at BBC Online, and details of global warming from the World Wide Fund for Nature:
www.opec.org
www.bbc.co.uk/news/world/costoffuel
www.wwf.org

Further reading For a full treatment, read:
Begg, Fischer, Dornbusch: *Economics, 6/e*, McGraw-Hill, 2000
  Chapter 1 (oil prices)
  Chapter 10 (cartels & OPEC)
  Chapter 16 (externalities)

Alternatively, for a streamlined introduction, read:
Begg, Fischer, Dornbusch: *Foundations of Economics*, McGraw-Hill, 2001
  Chapter 1-1 (oil prices)
  Chapter 3-3 (cartels)
  Chapter 5-1 (externalities)

4 European monetary union: a progress report

European monetary union, a permanently fixed exchange rate agreement with a single central bank setting a single interest rate, was launched in January 1999. Of the 15 member countries, 11 initially participated—the exceptions were the UK, Denmark, Greece, and Sweden. Greece has subsequently joined. The new currency, the euro, will begin circulating in January 2002.

Optimists forecast that a single currency would help integrate member states by eliminating market segmentation caused by both conversion costs between currencies and uncertainty about the exchange rate at which conversion would occur. The euro would help create a unified single market, capable of meeting the United States on a level playing field.

Part of this hope has indeed been fulfilled. In particular, European shareholders are now better diversified across countries. Previously, national regulations, for example on pension funds, prevented substantial buying of foreign equities and bonds. Lawyers thought this guaranteed safety for investors in these funds. Economists thought the restrictions were crazy and made the funds less safe, by forcing them to invest only in domestic assets. Now Portuguese pension funds and insurance companies can happily hold French and German shares, as Portuguese lawyers no longer regard these shares as denominated in a foreign currency.

In other ways, European financial integration is proceeding painfully slowly, both inside and outside the eurozone. Each country's national champions, the leading firms in banking, insurance and so on, want the common rules written to preserve their existing advantages. Reaching any agreement is taking a long time.

Maastricht criteria
Laid down in 1991, these were conditions that EU member countries had to meet before being judged eligible for entry to monetary union. Greece joined late because it had not met the criteria at the time the eurozone was launched.

Risk pooling
Diversification means not putting all your eggs in one basket. Savers benefit from holding a wider portfolio than merely assets in the domestic currency.

EU and euro differ The UK is now one of three EU members not in the eurozone. Many issues of closer integration, such as taxes and regulation, have nothing to do with monetary union.

The London and Frankfurt stock exchanges failed to merge and create a global player. They could not agree on whose contract law to use. The euro had nothing to do with the wish to merge or the failure to achieve it.

UK concerns about membership

UK concerns about membership of the eurozone are less about these microeconomic issues than about macroeconomic sovereignty. They can be divided into three categories. First, there is outright nationalism. 'We won the war and should not give away our sovereignty now.' This invites the obvious rejoinders that (a) having won the war, the UK has comprehensively lost the peace, being overtaken in living standards by many EU countries in the post-war period; and (b) financial market integration has already deprived nation states of much of their monetary independence.

The Bank of England has often expressed concern about both the strength of sterling, which makes exporting harder, and the extent of the boom in house prices in the south-east of the UK. It wanted to cut interest rates to help exporters, but also to raise interest rates to cool off house prices. It could not do both. Had sterling been less sensitive to interest differentials between the UK and its partners, the Bank of England might have done more to let the steam out of the housing boom.

The second concern is that because the UK economy is not yet highly correlated with the economies of continental Europe, joining the euro now would be premature. This is partly the legacy of 1992: the UK left the ERM and began a policy of expansion, and most other EU countries stayed in the ERM and continued with restrictive policies. The two business cycles are still out of line. One of Gordon Brown's economic tests for UK entry to the eurozone is that business cycles should have become harmonized.

The second concern also reflects a worry that the UK economy is structurally different from its continental European counterparts, and hence will need different interest rate treatment even after past ripples have evened out. This used to be true, but closer economic integration with continental Europe—now the UK's major trading partner—is steadily eroding this objection. When the timing is right is nevertheless a matter of judgement.

If the UK becomes more like its eurozone counterparts, and is therefore content to follow a similar monetary policy, the third concern is that monetary policy in the eurozone might be less competently pursued than the monetary policy of the Bank of England.

This was not always the case. During the difficult period of the mid-1970s, UK inflation grew to over 20 per cent a year. Few dispute that the Bundesbank pursued a superior policy during that period.

However, UK monetary policy has now been placed on a sound footing. The Bank of England has been given operational independence to decide how to set interest rates to meet the goal prescribed by government: keeping inflation in check. So-called 'inflation targeting' does not imply a neglect of the needs of the real economy—output and jobs—since the main reason inflation increases is that demand has been allowed to get ahead of full-capacity output. Keeping demand close to that level is a recipe for delivering low inflation.

Chancellor of the Exchequer, Gordon Brown

ERM Exchange rate mechanism of fixed but occasionally adjustable exchange rates within the EU. It lasted from 1979 to 1998. The UK joined in 1990 and left in 1992.

Cross-country correlations Countries specializing in similar products may have similar cycles. If both need the same policy, there is no cost in sharing a single currency. There is evidence that the act of joining a currency zone enhances output correlation.

Inflation targets The Bank of England's job is to keep UK inflation between 1.5 and 2.5 per cent a year. When the Bank foresees higher inflation, it raises interest rates.

ECB The European Central Bank, which sets the single interest rate. Currently, the ECB has a Governing Council on which each member state is represented, and a smaller Executive Board.

Not only has UK monetary policy improved, but there is also some concern that the new European Central Bank (ECB) has yet to convince markets that it is fully on top of the job.

Early days in the eurozone

One thing people point to is the steady reduction in the euro exchange rate since the euro began life at the start of 1999. The first chart shows the steady evaporation of its international value against the US dollar. Euro members feel this reflects a lack of confidence in the euro and in the ECB, which runs monetary policy.

This view is too simplistic. The second chart shows little trend in the exchange rate between sterling and the euro. In short, the first chart should be viewed more as the strength of the dollar than as the weakness of the euro. It is then a bit unfair to blame the ECB.

It is also inconsistent to take the view, often espoused by British eurosceptics, that a fall in the pound would be good for UK exports (and hence the UK should retain monetary independence to be able to accomplish this), whereas the ECB should be blamed for presiding over a fall in the value of the euro, which presumably has a beneficial effect on exports from the eurozone.

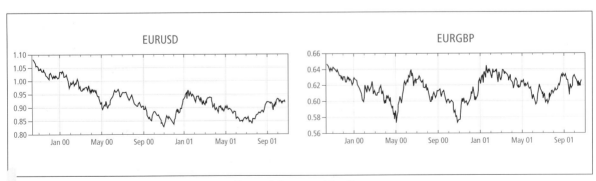

The fluctuations of the Euro against the US Dollar and the Pound Sterling

Nor is it especially helpful to examine the evolution of the euro from January 1999 onwards. That is certainly the date at which the eurozone began. However, what examination of this period misses is that the constituent currencies of the euro had experienced a strong appreciation in the months before the start of the eurozone. The euro was therefore overvalued when it was born. Some of its subsequent fall has been a useful correction to 'market exuberance' about the advance prospects of the eurozone.

Still room for improvement

These are important caveats to the usual pessimism about the euro's performance. Nevertheless, the ECB could do better, and probably will. Institutionally, it began with a great handicap. It wanted to emphasize continuity with the practices of the Bundesbank (BUBA), which had been a great success, but the ECB was no longer a German monopoly. In the event, it opted for a compromise that has not served it well.

The Bundesbank had placed great stress on the evolution of the stock of money as an indicator of future inflation. Many other countries had found this indicator somewhat unreliable. To emphasize its continuity with Bundesbank policy, the ECB announced that its monetary policy relied on the 'twin pillars' of an inflation forecast and the way the money stock evolved. When explaining its interest rate decisions, it has tried to justify its actions in terms of these twin pillars. Many people think it would be more transparent to explain its actions in terms of inflation targeting.

BUBA The Bundesbank, the German central bank. National central banks still exist in the eurozone, but they no longer set interest rates. Many central bank governors sit on the ECB's Governing Council.

Twin pillars The two planks on which ECB monetary decisions rest. The ECB looks at both its inflation projections and how the money stock is evolving.

The Deutsche Bundesbank, Frankfurt/Main

The ECB has now gone somewhat in this direction by making public its 'inflation projections'. However, these are an artificial construct since they are hypothetical projections on the assumption that interest rates remain unaltered. Sometimes the projections entail scenarios in which the ECB would clearly be driven to change interest rates in order to continue to fulfil its mandate of price stability.

By now there is an entire industry of ECB watchers, seeking to decode its true workings from its revealed actions and its public defence of them. In general, the consensus is that the ECB has not done badly, even if its explanations of its own actions have not always been as transparent as they might have been.

Just as an organisation (or a person) never gets a second chance to make a first impression, so it can never inherit a track record. The ECB is having to

For sale signs proliferate as the Notting Hill housing boom raged

build its own. So far, it has displayed unwillingness to move interest rates as frequently as its counterparts in the United States and the UK. We are still waiting to discover whether this reflects a deliberate process of consensus building in this young institution, or whether it reflects a greater diversity of interest that entails strains within the eurozone. However, the next time someone tells you that an Irish boom plus a German slump adds up to a headache for the ECB, remind them of the Bank of England's migraine over the Rover and Vauxhall implosion that coincided with a crazy housing boom in Notting Hill. Nobody said central banking was supposed to be easy.

Monetary union is a response to a loss of national sovereignty in monetary policy. If the sensitivity of cross-border flows of money is sufficiently high, it no longer makes sense to think of having separate national monetary policies. As yet, other cross-border flows are less of a problem, but they do exist. Even where they continue to be handled by national governments, they are the subject of considerable intergovernmental discussion. One such issue is the cross-border movement of people.

Useful websites   For material in this section:
  www.bankofengland.co.uk
  www.ecb.int
  www.federalreserve.gov

Further reading   For a full treatment, read:
  Begg, Fischer, Dornbusch: *Economics, 6/e*, McGraw-Hill, 2000
    Chapter 34 (International monetary system)
    Chapter 35 (European integration)

Alternatively, for a streamlined introduction, read:
  Begg, Fischer, Dornbusch: *Foundations of Economics*, McGraw-Hill, 2001
    Chapter 10-2 (International monetary system)
    Chapter 10-3 (Economics of EMU)

5 Asylum and immigration: getting beyond the rhetoric

In most rich countries, immigration is the subject of acute political controversy. Sometimes the public debate seeks to distinguish refugees and economic migrants. The former arrive seeking asylum because they face political or religious persecution in their country of origin. The latter simply hope to raise their living standards by switching the country in which they live. Even the societies ready to admit genuine asylum seekers are usually much more reluctant to offer unlimited entry to economic migrants.

This reluctance may be based on the consequence of immigration: altering a country's ethnic balance. Even in truly multicultural societies, rapid changes in the balance may cause difficulties. More frequently, however, the desire to limit economic immigration is based on fears that economic migrants will somehow be an economic burden on the existing population. They will take up welfare, have access to free health and education services, increase urban congestion, and make use of expensive training without necessarily promising to remain thereafter.

However, it is also possible that economic migrants are those who show initiative and respond to market incentives (after all, they appear to be responding to the incentive to relocate). Perhaps they will become productive workers and make important contributions to tax revenues. Any assessment of the impact of economic migrants needs to be based on solid empirical research. A recent survey of such research (see OECD *Economic Outlook*, December 2000) concludes that inflows of economic migrants lead to small overall gains for the host country. Immigrants have little impact on the unemployment of a country's inhabitants; indeed, they provide an increasingly valuable supply of labour and tax revenue as demographic trends in Europe, the United States, and Japan lead to ageing host populations in which labour supply and the tax base would otherwise shrink.

Refugee Someone escaping persecution by moving to another country.

Economic migrant Someone moving to another country to improve their living standards.

Asylum The act of granting sanctuary to a refugee.

Demographic trends Demography is the study of population. OECD countries now have low birth and death rates, and hence populations in which the proportion of elderly people is rising.

In principle, this process could eventually proceed to the point at which economic immigrants are shown the red carpet rather than the cold shoulder.

The current scale of immigration

Table 5-1 shows the level of immigration per 1000 inhabitants of each host country in the OECD. Switzerland and Germany are most open to immigration; in particular, they have a well-organized system of temporary immigrants or guest workers which they use both to meet labour market bottlenecks during booms and to fill jobs that their rich citizens no longer wish to do themselves. Japan, France, Finland and Hungary are least open to immigration. The UK is slightly above average.

As well as examining the annual inflow of immigrants, researchers have also considered the stock of foreign-born people now resident as a result of past immigration. In this respect, British Commonwealth countries—Australia, Canada and the UK itself—stand out as having large stocks of previous immigrants. In Australia, 21 per cent of the population is foreign or foreign born; in the UK it is 19 per cent, and in Canada it is 17 per cent. These figures compare with 10 per cent in the United States, and an average of 5 per cent in the EU.

Table 5-1   OECD: immigrants per 1000 residents, 1998

Country	No.	Country	No.
Switzerland	10.6	Sweden	4.1
Germany	7.5	Denmark	3.8
Norway	6.0	Italy	2.6
Canada	5.8	USA	2.4
Netherlands	5.4	Japan	2.1
Belgium	5.2	France	1.9
UK	5.1	Finland	1.6
Australia	4.2	Hungary	1.2

Source: OECD *Economic Outlook*, 2000.

Economic migration is a response to economic incentives. Such immigrants supply themselves because, by working with better capital and more skilled workers than they would at home, they expect to be more productive and earn more. Immigrants are demanded by the host country because they augment the supply of scarce resources, most obviously labour. To the extent that rich countries have abundant skilled labour but comparatively less unskilled labour, we might expect rich countries to 'demand' immigrants who augment the pool of unskilled labour. Table 5-2 confirms that this is largely the case. In most countries, the educational qualification of immigrants is lower than the average level of the host population.

The impact of immigration

Do migrants increase unemployment? There is no statistical evidence that they do. In particular, there is no cross-country correlation between the extent of migration, current or cumulative, and national unemployment rates.

Economic theory suggests that there may be some effect on wages. An increase in the supply of unskilled labour will bid down equilibrium wages for this type of labour. This benefits all those who employ unskilled labour

Reasons for economic migration Migrants rarely intend to live off welfare, even though this may be more money than they receive by working in their country of origin. By gaining access to better equipment and more skilled colleagues, a migrant's productivity will increase.

Cross-country correlation Similar movement in two variables from country to country. Thus a positive cross-country correlation of migration and unemployment would mean that countries that had taken lots of migrants also had high rates of unemployment. This is not what the evidence shows.

Table 5-2 Educational attainment, 1995–98 average
(% of group with only primary or lower secondary education)

	Immigrants	Host population
Canada	22	23
France	63	33
Germany	49	13
Italy	47	56
Sweden	31	20
UK	65	44
USA	35	16

Source: OECD *Economic Outlook*, December 2000.

or consume the products that such labour helps to produce, but reduces wage incomes of those who were already in such jobs. Thus although the nation as a whole probably benefits, the particular groups in labour market competition with immigrants may be adversely affected. As in other areas of change, the losers shout loudly and may force politicians to take notice. Nevertheless, most empirical studies conclude that induced effects on wages and employment are generally quite small.

Are immigrants a burden on the taxpayer because they receive large amounts of welfare and free public services? Since it takes time to find work and develop skills, immigrants may initially make net demands on the public finances. However, empirical studies that follow immigrants over time generally conclude that the present value of their contributions to the public finances through taxes exceed the present value of what they take out (see OECD, *Trends in International Migration*, 1997). As immigrants increasingly prosper, they repay with interest the public support they initially received.

As the baby boomers of the 1950's and 1960's retire then the result will be a much smaller labour force supporting a much larger retired population

How valuable could immigrants become?

In the late 20th century, the birth rate in rich countries fell. Simultaneously, life expectancy increased with better nutrition and medical advances. The consequence has been a dramatic change in the age structure of the population. Already schools and universities are experiencing the consequences of there being fewer young people than before. Soon the labour market will experience the same effect. Meanwhile, the baby boomers born in the 1950s and 1960s are well on the way to retirement. By 2010 the effect will be clearly visible: a smaller labour force supporting a much larger retired population.

In the following decades this effect will intensify, with two consequences. First, per capita GDP will fall: normal technical progress and capital accumulation will be offset by an absolute decline in the labour force. Second, the tax burden on young workers is likely to increase as the public finances strain to cope with the pension and health demands of the ageing population. In these circumstances, inflows of potential workers will be welcomed as an injection of taxpaying workers that eases the conflict emerging between young and old.

Thus attitudes to economic migrants are likely to change in the coming decades. Could the scale of immigration be sufficient to overcome the two adverse trends cited above? The United Nations has estimated[1] that a modest increase in immigration levels might maintain the size of OECD working-age populations at current levels. Although this might be sufficient to deal with part of the problem, i.e. the scarcity of young workers, it would not be nearly enough to deal with the harder part of the problem, i.e. the increasing number of people living well into old age, people who consume but no longer produce.

Table 5-3 shows the dramatic increase in flows of net inward migration that would be needed to maintain the share of old people in the population at its current level. Moreover, even if this could be achieved, the consequence would be a tripling of EU population between 2000 and 2050. This is simple arithmetic. If we already know the number of old people will triple, and we wish to prevent the population becoming lopsided, the number of young people will also have to triple. Hence total population triples. Of course, this would place massive strains on other resources. Think of the congestion, the

Per capita GDP GDP is national output. Per capita GDP is national output divided by population.

Working age The working-age population is made up of people aged between 18 and 65.

Age structure The fraction of the population in each age group. Stabilizing the age structure means keeping these fractions constant. Since the elderly will grow in absolute numbers, so must other groups if the structure is to stay the same. This cannot come from births (too few). It could come from migration. However, a huge rise in total population would over-stretch other resources.

---

[1] United Nations (2000). *Replacement migration: is it a solution to declining and ageing populations?*, Department of Economics and Social Affairs, New York.

Table 5-3 Stabilizing the current age structure, 2000–2050

	2000	2020	2030	2040	2050
Required inflow of migrants (thousand)					
EU	5	10	18	17	17
USA	0	15	15	6	30
Japan	6	4	5	21	18
Consequent total population (million)					
EU	400				1220
USA	280				1060
Japan	180				800

Source: OECD *Economic Outlook*, December 2000.

additional public infrastructure and the amount of extra productive capital that would be needed. Since this is implausible, in practice immigration will not proceed on such a massive scale. But it will increase from current levels.

Summing up

Current immigration policy in rich countries often hinges on the distinction between asylum seekers and economic migrants. Politicians often draw a distinction, arguing that rich countries are morally obliged to allow immigration by people who are persecuted but face no such obligation to allow in economic migrants who can be expected to be a burden on the host country. Much effort then goes into the process that determines whether a potential immigrant has genuinely been persecuted or should simply be viewed as a migrant responding to economic incentives.

It is not for us to judge whether economic immigration causes social problems; that is a matter for sociologists not economists. However, the widespread presumption that economic migrants cause a purely economic burden is unproved by existing empirical research. Indeed, on balance, the evidence appears to go the other way. Moreover, known demographic trends will only enhance the benefit of economic migrants in the future. At some point, electorates and politicians may therefore cease to distinguish between asylum seekers and economic migrants for the purpose of favouring the former against the latter.

Every taxi driver and stand-up comedian thinks they can pontificate about economics without any formal training. But few of them would go to a surgeon who had no training. When the chips are down, we want the expert. Analysis by the best economists commands respect because it follows the scientific method. It formulates hypotheses and then gathers evidence in order to test theories against the facts. There is not a Nobel Prize for taxi driving, but there is one for Economic Science.

Useful websites For material in this section see those of the OECD, the United Nations, and the UK Home Office:
www.oecd.org
www.un.org
www.homeoffice.gov.uk

Further reading For a full treatment, read:
Begg, Fischer, Dornbusch: *Economics, 6/e*, McGraw-Hill, 2000
   Chapter 11 (labour markets)
   Chapter 12 (discrimination)
   Chapter 31 (economic growth)

Alternatively, for a streamlined introduction, read:
Begg, Fischer, Dornbusch: *Foundations of Economics*, McGraw-Hill, 2001
   Chapter 4-1 (labour markets)
   Chapter 4-2 (discrimination)
   Chapter 11-1 (economic growth)

6 Economics— A Nobel Science

What is the Nobel Prize?

Alfred Nobel, a Swedish industrialist and the inventor of dynamite, died in 1896. By then he had amassed a large fortune, and he left some of it to fund annual 'Nobel Prizes' to recognize outstanding achievement in the arts, sciences and political life. People win Nobel Prizes for Literature, Peace, Medicine, Physics and Chemistry. The Nobel Prize in Economics is not one of the original five prizes founded by Nobel. It was established in 1968 by Sweden's central bank, the Riksbank, to commemorate Nobel, mark the Riksbank's tercentenary and confirm the importance of economics as a serious subject for scientific research.

Riksbank The central bank of Sweden, analogous to the Bank of England. Like its British counterpart, the Riksbank is operationally independent and pursues an inflation target specified by the government.

The Rijksbank in Stockholm, Sweden

Alfred Bernard Nobel (1833–1896)

Optimal income tax rates Mirrlees's theory of incentives gave rise to a whole new branch of economics—how contracts should reflect imperfect information. Another question that interested him was how progressive the income tax system should be when the government knows that high tax rates are good for redistribution but bad for work incentives.

James Meade

Jim Mirrlees

Past winners

Past British winners of the Nobel Prize in Economics include James Meade and Jim Mirrlees. Meade's research included effects of taxation and the determinants of international trade. Meade donated his prize money to help found the prestigious Institute for Fiscal Studies, which has subsequently produced a stream of high-quality research on issues in fiscal policy (www.ifs.org.uk). Its regular journal, *Fiscal Studies*, is a useful source of material on the UK policy debate. Mirrlees helped to pioneer the theory of incentives: how, in the presence of imperfect information, a principal should design contracts for agents to induce hard-to-monitor agents to behave as closely as possible in the way the principal would ideally like. Another past winner, Amartya Sen, an Indian, is now Master of Trinity College, Cambridge. Sen is one of the world's leading authorities on poverty and famine.

Other past winners of the Nobel Prize in Economics include Americans Milton Friedman (famous for work on inflation and monetarism, but also the author of groundbreaking early work on consumer spending), Paul Samuelson (whose extensive contributions ranged from trade theory to welfare economics), Bob Solow (who developed the modern theory of growth) and Robert Lucas (who pioneered the theory of how expectations are formed, and also worked on long-run economic growth). Past winners of the Nobel Prize can be found at www.nobel.se/economics.

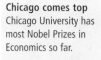

Chicago comes top
Chicago University has most Nobel Prizes in Economics so far.

Milton Friedman

Paul Samuelson

Robert Lucas

Bob Solow

Daniel L. McFadden

The 2000 Nobel Prize in Economics

The 2000 prize (now worth about £600,000) was won by two American economists, James Heckman and Daniel McFadden, for developing ways to study how and why people make decisions about where to live, work and study. Heckman and McFadden combine microeconomic theory and the statistical analysis of detailed data. They invented procedures that are very general and have many other applications. (See websites: www.harrisschool.uchicago.edu/faculty/fac_heckman.html; www.elsa.berkeley.edu/users/mcfadden/index.html)

Discrete choice analysis
McFadden showed that when people have to make all or nothing choices, it is best to model probabilities of making each choice. Each probability can depend on the usual economic suspects—price, income, preference—and small changes in these determinants can lead to small changes in the probabilities, for example, in taking the bus or the car.

McFadden pioneered the analysis of 'all or nothing' choices, such as whether to go by bus or not, which cannot be analysed in the same way as continuous choices, such as whether to have 1.5, 1.6 or 1.7 litres of beer. The citation from the Royal Swedish Academy of Sciences read:

> *The microeconometric methods developed by Heckman and McFadden are now part of the standard tool kit, not only of economists, but also of other social scientists. (www.nobel.se/announcements/2000/economics)*

McFadden, of the University of California at Berkeley, showed how the probability of making a decision (for example, to travel by bus or by car) could be theoretically and empirically related both to personal characteristics, such as age, income, education of the person making the decision, and to attributes of the products, such as the cost of a journey or the time it takes. A stunned and surprised McFadden told Reuters by telephone from his home in California:

> *In retrospect, it all seems blindingly obvious, but at the time it wasn't. What I did, beginning in the 1960s, was to take the economic theory of self-interest, which governs economic behaviour, and apply it to life's big decisions: when to get married, how many children to have, what occupation to choose.*

His work was important in designing the San Francisco metro (the Bay Area Rapid Transit System) as well as telephone services. It is also used to estimate the demand for energy and housing for the elderly. He devoted his share of the prize money to his farm in northern California's wine country.

The other winner in 2000 was James Heckman, of the University of Chicago. Heckman's work includes the recognition that investigators sometimes have to work with data that constitute a biased sample, unrepresentative of the whole population. Among other things, he designed statistical methods to evaluate the effect of job-market training programmes and employment subsidies, and how the length of unemployment affects an individual's chances of subsequently getting a job. 'I'm honoured and flattered,' said Heckman, who confessed he did not know which of his works won him the prize. Bertil Holmlund of Uppsala University, a member of the Nobel Prize committee, told a news conference in Stockholm:

Heckman has improved our understanding of the labour market and salaries. He is at the forefront of our understanding of the welfare system in the US.

The San Francisco metro (the Bay Area Rapid Transit System)

BART When the Bay Area Rapid Transit, or BART, was launched, San Francisco offered a prize for the best advertising slogan. The winner?

Humphrey GO BART!

James Heckman

Sample selection bias
You want a burglar alarm but are put off by reading that people with alarms have the same chance of being robbed as other people.

Wrong! People fit alarms only because they begin with an above-average chance of being burgled. If alarms get you back to average, they are working quite well. People with alarms are not a random sample of the population but a high-risk group. Heckman worked out how to analyse this properly.

Heckman and McFadden have been friends and colleagues for years. Heckman said:

> I am very honoured to share the prize with him. He was never my teacher in the classroom, but in life he taught me a lot. So much of my work is based on his models.
>
> Sources: www.yahoo.com/news; www.bbc.co.uk

Useful website www.nobel.se/economics

7 Final postscript: after the terrorists struck...

There is no conclusion, no place to stop. Even as we go to print, another huge development in world political and economic affairs has taken place and we are already reaching for the tool in our back pocket....

In the week after the terrorist attacks on New York and Washington, world stock markets plummeted nearly 20 per cent. Airlines and insurance companies were especially badly hit. Nor was the gloom confined to US airlines: for example, British Airways shares fell 50 per cent within two weeks.

Central banks, of course, responded by cutting interest rates. Initially, the Federal Reserve and the European Central Bank cut by 0.5 per cent and the Bank of England by 0.25 per cent. How can we square the huge pessimism of stock markets with the relatively small initial response by central bankers?

The Bank of England noted that its formal mandate is purely to maintain low inflation. It has no specific brief to stabilize output or confidence. With the effects of higher oil prices continuing to feed into inflation, and the possibility that tension in the Middle East may curtail oil supplies and drive oil prices even higher, the Bank felt unable to go beyond a small initial gesture.

Central banks have also learned the lessons from Japan that we discussed in Section 1. Once interest rates get close to zero, the main weapon of monetary policy has been used up. Bad as things looked after the terrorist attack, policy makers may have wished to keep some of their powder dry in case things got even worse later.

US airlines went scrambling to the government for subsidies. The private sector argues strongly for windfall subsidies during a crisis, yet is strangely resistant to windfall taxes during any bonanza.

Stock market falls
These reflect the expected stream of dividends for the foreseeable future. Big falls in share prices of airlines imply more than a temporary slump in the number of airline passengers.

Permanent extra costs include likely additional security. World tension will probably also keep fuel prices high for a long time.

Passing higher costs on in higher plane fares will then also reduce demand for travel.

A level playing field? Strategic competition in the global economy means that actions by one country may affect firms elsewhere.

Early indications are that much of any US subsidy may go to Boeing, the plane maker, rather than to airlines, the plane users. Should the European plane maker Airbus now seek equivalent help from European governments? Although Airbus has recently been flourishing, any sustained slump in air travel will cause huge excess capacity. Orders for new planes will dry up. If Europe allows Airbus to go under, Boeing will become the only major plane maker in the world.

Competition authorities are unlikely to find that a comfortable prospect. Some day, air travel will recover, and then Boeing's monopoly power would be vast. Europe may prefer to help Airbus through any tough times ahead, and the US government, so quick to help Boeing, will find it had to object. Nor should it—US consumers also benefit from competition between plane makers.

For the rivalry between Boeing and Airbus, and the role of subsidies, see:
Begg, Fischer, Dornbusch: Economics, 6/e, McGraw-Hill, 2000
Chapter 18

Or, for a streamlined introduction read:
Begg, Fischer, Dornbusch: Foundations of Economics, McGraw-Hill, 2001
Chapter 6-1

The Airbus Industrie A319/A321 assembly line in Hamburg

8 Conclusion

Our ancient ancestor who invented the wheel probably grinned for days after making his discovery—so useful, and so obvious. The best ideas are simple, widely applicable, and lead us on to further new challenges.

Even after years of study and research, economics still makes us grin. It helps us make sense of the world in which we find ourselves. For this reason, economics is not something to put away between lectures, but something to carry round in a back pocket, like a Swiss army knife—portable and multipurpose.

The *Postscript* is intended to give you a helping hand as you practice using this tool. There will always be tomorrow, with new issues to be analysed, but your tool has many blades, and is up to most of the tasks ahead. Learn to use it well.

9 Economic and Financial indicators

The 4 tables overleaf are reproduced from The Economist issues of 23rd September 2000 and 22nd September 2001. They show a variety of economic and financial data. Take a look at the figures—what conclusions can you draw?

Stockmarkets Market indices September 20th 2000

	Sept 20th 2000	2000 High	2000 Low	One week	Record High	% change on December 31st 2000 Local Currency	% change on December 31st 2000 In $ terms
Australia (All Ordinaries)	3,206.5	3,330.4	2920.0	-2.4	-3.7	+1.7	-15.9
Austria (ATX)	1,169.4	1,236.1	1,029.4	-1.2	-32.7	-2.4	-17.5
Belgium (Bel 20)	2,975.1	3,340.4	2532.2	-2.4	-19.2	-10.9	24.7
Britain (FTSE 100)	6,279.9	6,930.2	5,994.6	-3.1	-9.4	-9.4	20.5
Canada (Toronto Composite)	10,813.1	11,388.8	8,114.2	+0.6	-5.1	+28.5	+25.8
Denmark (KBX)	982.6	1,013.6	755.1	+0.2	-3.1	+26.8	+6.9
France (SBF 250)	4,073.6	4,390.7	3,512.9	-2.5	-7.2	+6.9	-9.6
Germany (Xetra DAX)	6,765.2	8,065.0	6,474.9	-3.5	-16.1	-2.8	-17.8
Italy (BCI)	1,994.1	2,182.3	1,666.4	-3.4	-8.6	+9.8	-7.2
Japan (Nikkei 225)	16,458.3	20,833.2	15,667.4	+1.7	-57.7	-13.1	-16.3
(Topix)	1,520.7	2,507.6	1,450.9	+2.5	-47.3	-11.7	-14.9
Netherlands (AEX)	664.4	701.6	612.4	-1.9	-5.3	-1.0	-16.3
Spain (Madrid SE)	1,011.5	1,146.2	952.1	-2.7	-11.8	+0.3	-15.2
Sweden (Affarsvarlden Gen)	5,808.6	6,960.6	5,176.3	-1.3	-16.6	+5.6	-8.5
Switzerland (Swiss Market)	7,831.8	8,377.0	6,781.4	-2.5	-6.9	+3.5	-7.1
United States (DJIA)	10,687.9	11,723.0	9,796.0	-4.4	-8.8	-7.0	-7.0
(S&P 500)	1,451.3	1,527.5	1,333.4	-2.3	-5.0	-1.2	-1.2
(Nasdaq Comp)	9,897.4	5,048.6	3,164.6	+0.1	-22.8	-4.2	-4.2
Europe (FTSE Eurotop 300)	1,616.0	1,705.0	1,472.5	-1.7	-5.2	+2.1	-13.7
Euro area (FTSE Ebloc100)	1,461.5	1,550.5	1,277.7	-2.2	-5.7	+5.5	-10.8
World (MSCI)	1,308.4	1,448.8	1,300.4	-4.7	-9.7	na	-7.9
World bond market Saloman	418.2	440.0	414.8	-0.5	-9.1	na	-4.3

From *the Economist*, with permission

Stockmarkets Market indices September 19th 2001

	Sept 19th 2001	2000 High	2000 Low	One week	Record High	% change on December 31st 2000 Local Currency	% change on December 31st 2000 In $ terms
Australia (All Ordinaries)	2,974.1	3,425.2	2,895.4	−2.5	−13.2	−5.7	−16.2
Austria (ATX)	1,114.4	1,245.8	1,052.2	−3.5	−35.8	+3.8	+2.8
Belgium (Bel 20)	2,483.4	3,030.4	2,483.4	−4.4	−32.6	−17.9	−18.7
Britain (FTSE 100)	4,721.7	6,334.5	4,721.7	−3.3	31.9	−24.1	25.4
Canada (Toronto Composite)	6,696.3	9,348.4	6,696.3	−5.0	−41.2	−25.0	−28.2
Denmark (KBX)	213.0	294.3	210.7	−4.7	−29.4	−19.5	−20.1
France (SBF 250)	2,495.2	3,820.2	2,495.2	−5.7	−43.2	−33.8	−34.5
(CAC 40)	3,888.9	5,998.5	3,888.9	−5.5	−43.8	34.4	35.0
Germany (Xetra DAX)	4,041.8	6,795.1	4,041.8	−6.8	−49.9	−37.2	−37.8
Italy (BCI)	1,211.1	1,948.4	1,202.8	−6.7	−44.5	−36.8	−37.4
Japan (Nikkei 225)	9,939.6	14,529.4	9,504.4	+3.4	−74.5	−27.9	29.8
(Topix)	1,038.1	1,441.0	863.4	+4.8	−64.0	−19.1	−21.3
Netherlands (AEX)	432.4	642.3	426.5	−4.5	−38.4	−32.2	−32.9
Spain (Madrid SE)	689.5	963.9	686.1	−4.0	−39.8	−21.7	−22.5
Sweden (Affarsvarlden Gen)	185.4	293.1	184.9	−4.2	−53.7	−33.3	−39.8
Switzerland (Swiss Market)	5,652.1	8,135.4	5,628.3	−3.2	−32.8	−30.5	−29.2
United States (DJIA)	8,759.1	11,337.9	8759.1	−8.8	−25.3	−18.8	−18.8
(S&P 500)	1,015.3	1,373.7	1015.1	−7.1	−33.5	−23.1	−23.1
(Nasdaq Comp)	1,527.7	2,859.2	1527.7	−9.9	−69.7	−38.2	−38.2
Europe (FTSE Eurotop 300)	1,113.0	1,545.5	1,078.1	−1.2	−34.7	−27.4	−28.1
Euro area (FTSE Ebloc100)	908.5	1,404.1	913.1	−5.6	−41.4	−34.7	−35.4
World (MSCI)	907.6	1,249.2	921.0	−4.4	−37.4	na	−25.7
World bond market Saloman	456.5	451.0	420.6	+1.8	−0.7	na	+2.8

From *the Economist*, with permission

Output, demand and jobs 2000
% change at annual rate

	GDP		Economist poll GDP forecasts		Industrial production	Retail sales (vol)	Unemployment % rate	
	1qtr	1year	2001	2002	1 year	1 year	Latest	year ago
Australia	+2.9	+4.7 Q2	+4.4	+3.7	+2.1 Q1	+4.7 Q2	6.4 Aug	7.1
Austria	+4.5	+3.9 Q1	+3.1	+2.9	+10.1 May	+10.8 May	3.2 Jul	3.8
Belgium	+5.5	+5.1 Q1	+3.9	+3.1	+8.0 Jul	+0.9 Apr	11.9 Aug	12.7
Britain	+3.6	+3.1 Q2	+2.9	+2.7	+1.1 Jul	+4.0 Aug	5.3 Jul	5.9
Canada	+4.7	+5.3 Q2	+4.5	+3.2	+7.1 Jun	+4.5 Jun	7.1 Aug	7.7
Denmark	−2.3	+1.7 Q1	+2.2	+2.2	Nil Jun	−1.6 Jun	5.4 Jul	5.6
France	+2.8	+3.3 Q2	+3.5	+3.3	+4.1 Jun	−1.6 Jul	9.7 Jul	11.2
Germany	+4.7	+3.1 Q2	+2.9	+2.9	+5.5 Jul	−2.2 Jul	9.5 Aug	10.5
Italy	+1.1	+2.6 Q2	+2.8	+2.7	−0.1 Jul	−1.7 Jun	10.7 Apr	11.5
Japan	+4.2	+0.8 Q2	+1.7	+2.0	+4.2 Jul	−0.3 Jul	4.7 Jul	4.8
Netherlands	+3.0	+4.1 Q2	+4.1	+3.5	+6.1 Jun	−4.1 Jun	2.5 Aug	3.2
Spain	+4.1	+3.9 Q2	+4.1	+3.5	+4.8 Jun	Na	14.2 Jul	15.3
Sweden	+5.5	+4.0 Q2	+4.2	+3.6	+11.6 Jun	+8.5 Jul	5.1 Aug	6.1
Switzerland	+2.5	+3.8 Q2	+3.2	2.5	+8.2 Q2	−4.0 Jul	1.8 Aug	2.4
United States	+5.3	+6.0 Q2	+5.1	3.3	+5.8 Aug	+7.0 Jul	4.1 Aug	4.2
Euro area	+3.7	+3.8 Q2	+3.5	3.1	3.8 Jun	+1.8 Jun	9.1 Jul	9.9

From *the Economist*, with permission

Output, demand and jobs 2001
% change at annual rate

	GDP		Economist poll GDP forecasts		Industrial production	Retail sales (vol)	Unemployment % rate	
	I qtr	I year	2001	2002	I year	I year	Latest	year ago
Australia	+3.6	+1.4 Q2	+2.5	+4.0	−1.4 Q1	+0.7 Q2	6.8 Aug	6.1
Austria	+1.6	+2.2 Q1	+1.7	+2.1	+8.0 Jun	−3.3 May	3.9 Aug	3.6
Belgium	−2.4	+1.7 Q2	+1.9	+2.4	+5.2 Jul	+5.3 Jun	11.6 Aug	11.9
Britain	+1.4	+2.1 Q2	+2.1	+2.6	−3.2 Jul	+6.3 Aug	5.0 Jul	503
Canada	+0.4	+2.1 Q2	+2.1	+2.8	−2.4 Jun	+3.5 Jun	7.2 Aug	7.1
Denmark	−4.6	+1.0 Q1	+1.3	+2.1	+4.4 Jun	+3.0 Jun	5.1 Jul	5.4
France	+1.0	+2.3 Q2	+2.2	+2.3	+2.3 Jun	−1.2 Jul	8.9 Jul	9.5
Germany	Nil	+0.6 Q2	+1.1	+1.9	−1.5 Jul	+0.9 Jul	9.3 Aug	9.4
Italy	−0.5	+2.0 Q2	+1.9	+2.2	+1.7 Jul	+0.1 Jun	9.5 Apr	10.7
Japan	-3.2	−0.7 Q2	−0.4	+0.5	−8.5 Jul	−2.4 Jun	5.0 Jul	4.7
Netherlands	+1.6	+1.5 Q2	+1.7	+2.5	+0.7 Jun	+1.8 May	2.0 Aug	2.5
Spain	+1.9	+2.9 Q2	+2.7	+2.8	−1.6 Jul	Na	13.0 Aug	13.9
Sweden	+1.3	+1.4 Q2	+2.0	+2.6	+2.6 Jun	+2.1 Jun	4.3 Aug	5.1
Switzerland	+1.7	+2.0 Q2	+1.6	+1.9	+5.1 Q1	+3.3 Jul	1.7 Aug	1.8
United States	+0.2	+1.2 Q2	+1.6	+2.6	−4.8 Aug	+3.8 Jul	4.9 Aug	4.1
Euro area	+0.2	+1.7 Q2	+1.8	+2.2	+1.4 Jun	+2.1 Jun	8.3 Jul	8.8

From *the Economist*, with permission